Marriage preparation workbook

A PRACTICAL GUIDE FOR COUPLES
CONSIDERING ENGAGEMENT OR MARRIAGE

DAVID SHERBINO

Renew: Marriage Preparation Workbook: A Practical Guide for Couples Considering Engagement or Marriage
Copyright ©2017 David Sherbino
All rights reserved
Printed in Canada
ISBN 978-1-927355-87-9 (soft cover)
ISBN 978-1-927355-88-6 EPUB

Published by:
Castle Quay Books
Burlington, Ontario
Tel: (416) 573-3249
E-mail: info@castlequaybooks.com   www.castlequaybooks.com

Edited by Marina Hofman Willard
Cover and interior design by Burst Impressions
Printed at Essence Printing, Belleville, Ontario

Scripture quotations are taken from the Holy Bible, New International Version®, NIV® Copyright ©1973, 1978, 1984, 2011 by Biblica, Inc.® Used by permission. All rights reserved worldwide.

All rights reserved. This book or parts thereof may not be reproduced in any form without prior written permission of the publisher.

Library and Archives Canada Cataloguing in Publication

Sherbino, David, author
    Marriage preparation workbook : a practical guide for couples considering or planning to get married / David Sherbino.

ISBN 978-1-927355-87-9 (softcover)

    1. Marriage--Handbooks, manuals, etc. I. Title.

HQ734.S54 2017   646.7'8   C2017-900343-7

Table of Contents

	PREFACE	5
01	*Introduction*	7
02	*Family* BACKGROUND	9
03	*Communication*	15
04	*Goals* AND ROLES	19
05	*Spiritual* LIFE	23
06	*Sexuality* AND FAMILY	27
07	*Finances*	31
08	MY *Commitment* IN MARRIAGE	37

PREFACE

This workbook is designed to help couples who are considering engagement or marriage to explore issues that are important in a marriage relationship.

The intent is for the couple to meet with a pastor or counsellor to discuss these important topics together. Each partner should have an individual copy of the manual and should answer the questions independently prior to each session.

The first chapter is an orientation to the pre-marriage counselling process designed to acquaint the pastor or counsellor with the couple and to cover details of the wedding ceremony. The following chapters present questions that cover the major areas of a couple's life. At the end of the workbook, there is an opportunity for the couple to speak directly to one another in terms of the commitment each person is prepared to make.

Enjoy the process.

—*David Sherbino*

Marriage preparation WORKBOOK

Love is patient, love is kind. It does not envy, it does not boast, it is not proud. It does not dishonor others, it is not self-seeking, it is not easily angered, it keeps no record of wrongs. Love does not delight in evil but rejoices with the truth. It always protects, always trusts, always hopes, always perseveres.

Love never fails. But where there are prophecies, they will cease; where there are tongues, they will be stilled; where there is knowledge, it will pass away. (1 Corinthians 13:4–8)

YOUR NAME:

_____

PARTNER'S NAME:

_____

TODAY'S DATE:

_____

01

This first set of questions provides the opportunity to introduce the pastor or counsellor to the couple. Whether you are well acquainted or strangers, it is helpful to discuss the basic details about the wedding service, the expectations of the pastor and the policies of the local church.

1) Background

These unique factors will contribute to your new relationship as husband and wife. Take a minute to discuss each item.

1. Education
2. Occupation
3. Hobbies and interests
4. Circumstances under which you met; what attracted you to each other
5. How long you have known each other

2) Church

If you desire to be married in a church, discuss the following:

1. Religious/church background
2. Why a church wedding is important

3) Pastoral Expectations

Discuss who will officiate at the wedding and what the expectations are of the officiator (pastor/priest).

4) Fee Structure

Note the fees for all services you require. Add to this list if needed.

1. Pastor
2. Wedding coordinator (if applicable)
3. Organist/musician
4. Technical services
5. Janitorial services
6. Rental of the church facilities

02 *Family* BACKGROUND

Families influence the way we perceive relationships. As two individuals from different backgrounds join their lives together in marriage, it is helpful to understand each person's family of origin. From your family of origin you have seen how your mother and father related to each other as husband and wife. Such awareness will enable you to perceive areas of commonality as well as differences, as demonstrated by your partner's family. This may include some aspects of your parents' marriage you would like to include and some aspects that you would want to change in your marriage relationship. Since there are many different family arrangements, feel free to adapt your responses to provide some insight into the situation you were raised in.

Friendship

Describe your parents' relationship in terms of the following:

Their friendship

_____
_____
_____
_____

Activities they shared together

_____
_____
_____
_____

Frequency of being together

Intensity of their relationship

Decision Making

How did they make decisions?

Was anyone the obvious leader in specific areas? Explain.

Spiritual Development and Training

What type of spiritual training did you receive? For example, did your parents take you to church and Sunday school, read the Bible to you or teach you how to pray? Be as specific as possible.

Who gave leadership in this area? Explain how this was done.
_____
_____
_____
_____

Money Management

Did both parents work outside the home? Describe their work involvement.
_____
_____
_____
_____

Who handled the finances?
_____
_____
_____
_____

Was there conflict over the use of money? How did they come to a decision about spending money?
_____
_____
_____
_____
_____
_____

Sexual Relationship

Did you observe affection or sexual expression between your parents? Describe what you observed.
_____
_____
_____
_____
_____

Did your parents openly discuss sexual issues with you? Who talked with you and what did they express?

_____
_____
_____
_____

How would you describe your parents' attitude toward sexuality?

_____
_____
_____
_____

Crisis

Was there any major crisis in your parents' marriage? Describe what this was.

_____
_____
_____
_____

If yes, how did this affect you? Be sure to explore how it impacted you emotionally.

_____
_____
_____

Qualities

Describe two positive qualities in your parents' marriage.

_____
_____
_____
_____

Describe two negative qualities in your parents' marriage.

_____
_____
_____
_____

Siblings

Describe the relationship you had with your siblings. Name each sibling and elaborate on your relationship with each one.

_____
_____
_____
_____

Which sibling had the greatest impact on you? Explain how this influenced you positively or negatively.

_____
_____
_____
_____

Connectedness

How would you describe your family?

❏ Emotionally connected (close)   or   ❏ Emotionally independent (distant)

❏ Flexible (open to change)   or   ❏ Rigid (resistant to change)

Comment on your choice.

_____
_____
_____

What do you want to bring from your family into this marriage?

_____
_____
_____

What do you not want to bring into this marriage from your family?

_____
_____
_____

02 *Family* BACKGROUND

Do you see similarities between your family and that of your partner?

Does your family approve of and support your plans for marriage?

03 Communication

This exercise is to help you explore issues that deal with communications. There may be some topics you have never discussed before.

Expressing Yourself

How do you express your anger? How does your partner react to this?
_____
_____
_____
_____
_____
_____

Does your partner have any habits that annoy or bother you? Describe what they are.
_____
_____
_____
_____

How do you show happiness?
_____
_____
_____
_____

Are you able to share your feelings when you are upset? How does your partner respond?

Do you ever act in a manner that gives you power and control over your partner? Sometimes people do this in a passive-aggressive manner.

Do you have similar interests or different interests?

Would your partner say one thing to you and mean another? If yes, can you give an example? How can this be improved?

Listening

How do you know that your partner is listening to you? Be specific.

03 Communication

Are you able to talk about problems without being overcome by your feelings?

Does your partner understand how you feel?

Apart from getting married, what do you think is the most important issue in your partner's life at this moment?

Affirmation

Does your partner ever put you down? If yes, give an example.

How do you respond?

Do you regularly compliment and affirm each other? Give some examples.

Changes

Is there any behaviour you would like to change in your partner?

What would you like him or her to do? How could this be done?

Is there any area of your relationship that you would like to change?

Do you have any fears or concerns about getting married? Please state them.

04 *Goals* AND ROLES

We have clearly defined roles in our places of employment, and many have established career goals. It is necessary to look at goals and roles in marriage if the relationship is going to grow and develop.

Goals

List five specific goals you hope to achieve over the next five years and the plan you have to accomplish each goal.

1 _____
2 _____
3 _____
4 _____
5 _____

Describe the ways your goals are similar to your partner's goals.
_____
_____
_____

Describe the ways your goals are different from your partner's goals.
_____
_____
_____
_____

How will you seek to resolve these differences?

Is your partner supportive in helping you attain your goals? Explain.

How do you like to spend your leisure time?

Are there leisure activities you like to do together and separately? Explain.

Roles

Describe how your parents perceived their roles in marriage. What role did each one assume?

Do both you and your partner expect to work outside the home? If so, what will this entail?

How will this affect your decisions regarding the division of labour in the home? Have you decided what each one will do?
_____
_____
_____
_____

What type of adjustments do you expect to make if both are working outside the home?
_____
_____
_____
_____

How do you make decisions as a couple?
_____
_____
_____
_____

What will you do if you come to an impasse or face significant disagreement?
_____
_____
_____
_____

Do you desire to maintain old friendships and contacts that might not necessarily involve your partner? Explain. How does your partner react to this?
_____
_____
_____
_____
_____
_____
_____

04 *Goals* AND ROLES

05 *Spiritual* LIFE

A Christian marriage assumes that you not only seek the blessing of God upon your marriage but that you also desire to grow as a couple in your relationship with God and with each other. The following questions invite you to explore a few significant issues that relate to your spiritual life.

Religious Upbringing

What is your church affiliation?

_____
_____
_____
_____

Present Practice

Do you regularly attend church? Describe your involvement. What does it mean to you?

_____
_____
_____
_____
_____
_____
_____

Marriage preparation WORKBOOK

Do you read Scripture and pray regularly? How important is this to you? Describe your routine.

What do you believe it means to be a Christian?

Write a brief statement describing your spiritual journey.

What are the spiritual issues you are working on in your life at this time?

What do you perceive to be the spiritual commitment of your partner? Describe.

Describe the components of a Christian marriage.

Who will give spiritual leadership in your home? Describe how this will work.

05 Spiritual LIFE

To what extent do you believe your life together must include active participation in church life?

_____
_____
_____
_____

Are there any differences between you and your partner in the area of your spiritual life? Do you foresee any conflict in this area? If you do, what will you do to resolve it?

_____
_____
_____
_____

Do you intend to raise your children in the same religious background that you were raised in? If you come from different traditions, what do you plan to do?

_____
_____
_____
_____

06 Sexuality AND FAMILY

God has made us sexual beings. In marriage, we have the opportunity for and joy of expressing our sexual feelings and desires in ways that will draw a couple closer together. People have different ways of expressing their desires, and thus these questions may help you to speak openly about yours.

Sexuality

Did your parents show affection to each other and to you? Describe their actions and words.

Did your parents openly talk about issues of a sexual nature?

How did you discover the basic information about sex?

Are you comfortable with the public display of affection? Describe what is acceptable to you.

What expressions of affection (words and actions) do you desire?

Are you able to talk openly to your partner about your sexual desires? Have you done so?

Who should take the initiative in sex? Why?

What type of sexual activity do you believe is appropriate in a marriage?

What type of sexual activity do you believe is not appropriate in a marriage?

What will you do to keep the romance alive in your marriage?

Family

06 Sexuality AND FAMILY

Have you decided on a method of birth control?

Do you desire to have children?

What size of a family would you like to have?

When would you like to start your family?

Are there things you want to accomplish before you begin a family?

How would you respond if your partner was unable to have children?

What expectations do you have about yourself in raising children?

What do you expect from your partner in this regard?

To what extent do you perceive your parents will be involved in raising your children?

Will this cause a problem?

Do you and your partner have different ideas about childrearing?

If you have children, do you plan to continue to work outside the home?

If you had a child with a disability, how do you think you would cope?

Do you think children will put a strain on your relationship? If yes, what will you do to cope with this?

07 Finances

Money plays an important role in your life together. However it can also be a source of great conflict. So use the following questions to explore some of your ideas about handling money.

Who was responsible for the financial management in your family home? Was this a satisfactory arrangement?
_____
_____
_____
_____

Who will handle the finances in your marriage?
_____
_____
_____
_____

Do you have outstanding debts? List them. Is this a concern?
_____
_____
_____
_____
_____
_____

How would you describe yourself in the way you handle money?

❑ Careful   ❑ Frugal   ❑ Spendthrift   ❑ Foolish

Now describe your partner.

❑ Careful   ❑ Frugal   ❑ Spendthrift   ❑ Foolish

Are you concerned about the amount of money you and your partner earn and the rising cost of living?

_____
_____
_____
_____

Will you share a joint account or maintain separate bank accounts?

_____
_____
_____
_____
_____

Will you have a weekly spending allowance?

_____
_____
_____
_____
_____

Does your partner have spending habits that bother you?

_____
_____
_____
_____
_____

Do you consult each other before you make a major purchase outside of your normal budget, such as a new television or a new computer?

_____
_____
_____
_____

07 Finances

Do you plan to donate to your church or a charity on a regular basis? Is this important to you?
_____
_____
_____
_____

Have you established a workable budget?
_____
_____
_____
_____

Do you have retirement goals?
_____
_____
_____
_____

What are you planning to do to achieve them?
_____
_____
_____
_____

Do you have a will? If not, do you perceive it to be necessary?
_____
_____
_____
_____

Basic Monthly Budget

Income Calculation

Income

Gross Salary (yours)	
Gross Salary (partner's)	
Other	
Other	
Other	
Total	

Deductions

Salary Deductions (yours)	
Salary Deductions (partner's)	
Other	
Total	

TOTAL INCOME

(Subtract total deductions from total income)

_____

Expenses Calculation

Housing

Rent/Mortgage	
Heating	
Water	
Electricity	
Cellphone	
Electronics (Cable, Internet, etc.)	
Repairs	
Other	
Total	

Transportation

Vehicle Payments	
Vehicle Gasoline	
Vehicle Maintenance	
License Renewal	
Parking	
Other	
Total	

Insurance

Life	
House	
Health	
Vehicle	
Other	
Total	

Medical

Medical Care	
Dental	
Prescription Drugs	
Therapy	
Other	
Total	

Donations

Church	
Charities	
Other	
Total	

Entertainment

Restaurants	
Plays, Movies, Theatre, etc.	
Sports/Hobbies	
Vacation	
Babysitter	
Other	
Total	

Education

Tuition	
Books	
Computer Equipment Supplies	
Other	
Total	

Personal

Allowance(s)	
Toiletries	
Clothing	
Barber/Beauty Salon	
Other	
Total	

Additional Expenses

Groceries, Household Items	
Savings	
Loan Repayments	
Credit Card Fees and Interest	
Miscellaneous/Petty Cash	
Other	
Total	

Summary

Total Income

TOTAL EXPENSES
(Add totals from 9 categories)

_____

BALANCE
(Subtract total expenses from total income)

_____

How does your resultant balance compare with that of your partner?

Where is there disagreement?

Are you satisfied with your resultant balance?

If you are not satisfied with this budget, what is your desired budget? What can you change to reach it? (Consider creating a revised budget with your desired budget goals for each item.)

08 MY *Commitment* IN MARRIAGE

This exercise is to help you look very practically and specifically at the relationship you are entering and what you are prepared to bring to that relationship.

Commitment Care Exercise

List 10 reasons why you want to marry this person.

1. ___
2. ___
3. ___
4. ___
5. ___
6. ___
7. ___
8. ___
9. ___
10. ___

What qualities do you bring to this marriage that will make it successful?

1. ___
2. ___
3. ___
4. ___
5. ___

Marriage preparation WORKBOOK

Read 1 Corinthians 13:4–7:

Love is patient, love is kind. It does not envy, it does not boast, it is not proud. It does not dishonor others, it is not self-seeking, it is not easily angered, it keeps no record of wrongs. Love does not delight in evil but rejoices with the truth. It always protects, always trusts, always hopes, always perseveres.

How will this passage apply to your marriage?

Write a marriage statement that includes "What I expect of myself" and "What I expect of my partner."

Renew
A BASIC GUIDE FOR A PERSONAL RETREAT

ISBN: 978-1-927355-72-9

In spite of all the good reasons we can think of, we can also come up with just as many good excuses not to take time to be away. In this new guide, David Sherbino helps you to get through any hindrances and identifies the many aspects and benefits of doing a personal retreat. It is a step-by-step guide that will help you with practical steps that allow you to develop and build your relationship with God, create an openness to God and learn to listen to what he has to say to you and be totally renewed.

Re:Connect
SPIRITUAL EXERCISES TO DEVELOP INTIMACY WITH GOD

ISBN: 978-1-927355-20-6

This book is filled with daily exercises and spiritual disciplines to help you draw close to God. It covers a period of seven weeks, and if you follow it carefully, you will notice a change in your spiritual practise and devotion.

Living, Dying, Living Forever
SPIRITUAL REFLECTIONS ON THE JOURNEY OF LIFE

ISBN: 978-1-927355-20-6

Living, Dying, Living Forever is designed as a workbook to help you explore the issues of living and dying as they relate to your relationship with God and with others. At the end of each chapter there are practical exercises you can follow to help you explore the issues on a personal level.

As you live out each day of the journey, these pages are designed to give you courage, hope and a perspective that embraces eternity.

www.ingramcontent.com/pod-product-compliance
Lightning Source LLC
Chambersburg PA
CBHW081356040426
42451CB00017B/3478